MANIFESTING YOUR BEST LIFE

A 90 Day Journal
To Help You Manifest Your Best Life

Jennifer Brown

Manifesting Your Best Life

Copyright © 2023 by Jennifer Brown

Printed in the United States of America

ISBN: 9798218186272

Published by Joseph's Ministry, LLC
(www.josephsministryllc.com)

Scripture quotations marked MSG are taken from THE MESSAGE, copyright © 1993, 2002, 2018 by Eugene H. Peterson. Used by permission of NavPress, represented by Tyndale House Publishers. All rights reserved.

Scripture quotations marked TPT are from The Passion Translation®. Copyright © 2017, 2018, 2020 by Passion & Fire Ministries, Inc. Used by permission. All rights reserved. ThePassionTranslation.com.

All rights reserved. No part of this publication may be reproduced, distributed, or transmitted in any form or by any means, including photocopying, recording, or other electronic or mechanical methods, without the prior written permission of the author except in the case of brief quotations embodied in critical reviews and certain other noncommercial uses permitted by copyright law.

This Journal Belongs To

_____

Date

_____

Introduction

Over the years, I have learned how to harness the power of my words and thoughts. Certainly, the process of time was needed to manifest the life I lead today. Before this transformation I was in a very unpredictable season, and my quality-of-life experience was stagnant and mundane. The vicious cycle of depression had truly taken up residency in my being, robbing me of my significance.

I prayed, often applying scripture to every prayer, but not seeing or feeling that my prayers were being answered. Did I lack faith? I literally would cry out to God asking, why am I not experiencing the joy, peace, and abundance, that I see others experiencing in their lives. Then I will become consumed with worry, and this left me spiritually frustrated, and angry with God.

My life changed dramatically in 2015. You can say it was the year of my "wakeup call" which will have to be a story for another day, but indeed it birth, this project you hold in your hands. The information that lies in these pages has been the blueprint to my manifested life and restoration of my soul.

I have seen too many people struggling and giving up on health, love, family, joy, and peace of mind. So, I knew I had to be intentional while partnering with God, seeking his wisdom, instructions, and guidance to fashion this journal.

I decree and declare this will be an Amos 9:13-15 journal. You will go from speaking it, to manifesting the life that you truly desire and ultimately receive every promise and provision God has made available to you.

Overflow of Blessings to You,

Jennifer Brown

"Yes indeed, it won't be long now." God's Decree.

"Things are going to happen so fast your head will swim, one thing fast on the heels of the other. You won't be able to keep up. Everything will be happening at once—and everywhere you look, blessings! Blessings like wine pouring off the mountains and hills. I'll make everything right again for my people Israel:

"They'll rebuild their ruined cities.
They'll plant vineyards and drink good wine.
They'll work their gardens and eat fresh vegetables.
And I'll plant them, plant them on their own land.
They'll never again be uprooted from the land I've given them."

God, your God, says so.

Amos 9:13-15 MSG

What is Manifestation?

Manifestation is believing you have what you cannot explicitly see yet. It is adopting the attitude of faith where you are moving as if what you asked for, prayed for, and written down, is already tangible and in your possession. Rather than "seeing is believing," manifestation is the idea that "believing is seeing."

You have the incredible potential to manifest anything you desire, - Wealth, optimum health, healing, money, love, cars, houses, and peace of mind… unfortunately many will not experience this level of manifested abundance because they fail to recognize or use their manifesting faith God has given them.

Now I'm sure you're wondering, "how can I just walk around believing that I have something that I don't have? Isn't there action required on my part?"

The answer is absolutely!

Action is required while you're manifesting:

1. You must first ask God, if what you are wanting to manifest, is it in alignment with your purpose and what He is doing for you in this season of your life.
2. The next action is to change how you think; your thoughts become your reality.
3. Be mindful of what you speak, your words are powerful.
4. Be aware of how you feel; feelings attract your experiences.
5. Have a spirit of gratitude; Gratitude is one of the most powerful tools of manifestation.
6. And BE CLEAR on WHAT YOU WANT and WRITE IT DOWN.

Oftentimes we want wonderful and ambitious things in life, but we don't think it feasible that we'll receive them. Words hold incredible power, and our feelings are the medium by which our desires will manifest faster. And when gratitude is put into motion it can bring about truly incredible things.

So, if you don't first create alignment between you and God, what you think, what you say, how you feel and be grateful; the disconnect will keep you stagnant.

The next steps required in manifesting, go in line with what you're believing in God for.

Prayer vs. Manifestation

Prayer and manifestation are two practices that have become increasingly popular in recent years, especially in the spiritual and personal development communities. While both are rooted in the desire to achieve a desired outcome, they differ in their approaches, beliefs, and benefits. Both are incredibly powerful tools that can help you create the life you want, but in two fundamentally different ways.

What is Prayer?
Prayer is a form of communication with God. This can be done through spoken words, thoughts, or written words. When you pray, you're asking for guidance, help, or protection. Like manifestation, prayer also involves setting your intention, but instead of focusing on what you want to attract, you focus on surrendering your desires to the Creator.

What is Manifestation?
Manifestation is the act of bringing something into existence. It's all about creating your reality through your thoughts and beliefs. What you focus on expands, so, if you want to manifest something in your life, you need to focus your thoughts and energy on it. This can be done through visualization or affirmations.

It's important to note that manifestation isn't just about attracting material possessions. Yes, you can use it to manifest a new car or a bigger house. However, manifestation can also be used to attract relationships, opportunities, and experiences. In short, manifestation is about creating your reality. You can use it to manifest anything you want, as long as you put in the work and focus on what you want to create.

Faith vs. Manifestation

Manifestation is often seen as a form of spiritual power. However, sometimes it is confused with faith. This can lead to misconceptions about both.

Manifestation

Manifestation, sometimes referred to as the "law of attraction", is a powerful method that uses thoughts to create reality. It is based on the idea that positive thoughts attract positive outcomes, while negative ones attract negative ones. Interestingly, many aspects of manifestation align with the teachings of Christianity and other religions. Although some people worry that manifesting takes God out of the equation, manifesting is perfectly acceptable to God as long as it is done with positive intentions, and you keep Him in the center of the process.

A manifestation is an approach to spiritual healing that focuses on the power of our thoughts and emotions. Its core concept is that like attracts like, so positive thoughts attract positive things, and negative thoughts attract negative things. The more powerful your thoughts and emotions are, the more likely you are to manifest.

Faith

Faith at its center is the belief in things we can't see that we through our experiences know to be true, i.e. the existence of God. Manifestation can be used as an outward expression of our inner faith that God will provide us with the things we desire and need in our lives to be happy and successful. Faith is action as well as belief. One can show faith not only by believing in what is to come but acting on what one believes will come. Faith is expressed by the way you live your life. The more you exercise it the more powerful it becomes in your life.

Christian believers believe in the power of the mind or practicing faith. This practice is similar to manifestation since it focuses on the power of our thoughts and emotions. In manifesting, our thoughts and emotions attract the things we desire. The more powerful our thoughts and emotions are, the more likely they are to manifest. This is similar to how faith works, the more faith we have in God, the more powerful we become in accessing the blessings and guidance of heaven.

Faith is actually the first step and building block that manifestation is based on. Manifestation involves thinking, believing, and acting in order to receive the things we desire. Faith is a willingness to let go of your fears and realign with the loving presence of God. However, like manifestation, it also requires thinking, believing, and acting to receive the blessings we desire.

Taking Action

How can faith and manifestation be used together? To start with, there are two ways to achieve your goals: action and faith. In order to manifest, you must have clearly defined goals that you are passionately committed to. In addition, you must really want to achieve them, refer back to your manifestation goals. While you must be willing to take general action to reach your goals, you must also have faith in yourself and in God that you will manifest what you are aiming for.

Taking action isn't necessary to be huge or monumental. Your actions will however show God that you are serious about manifesting. Faith without works is dead. The universe expects action, just as you would not trust a GPS navigation system if you don't move your car. Actions demonstrate your willingness to follow through on your dreams.

Manifestation uses the power of your thoughts and emotions to attract the things you desire. The law of attraction says that like attracts like, so positive thoughts will attract positive things, and negative thoughts will attract negative things. The more powerful your thoughts are, the more likely they will become reality.

God's Timing

If you're struggling to decide between God's timing and your faith, you're not alone. Millions of people face this question. They're waiting for God to fulfill a promise. In His time, your promise will be fulfilled. It's important to understand that God's timing isn't always syncopated with your own. For example, we should remember that God's time is different than ours. We often think we can live on our own schedule regardless.

This is where faith and having patience comes into play, that things will work out for you according to God's timing and grace.

In conclusion, having faith and praying as a practice is similar to manifestation since it focuses on the power of our thoughts and emotions. In manifesting, our thoughts and emotions attract the things we desire. The more powerful our thoughts and emotions are, the more likely they are to manifest. Faith is not a lack of power – it is a willingness to let go of your fears and realign with the loving presence of God. A manifestation is an approach to spiritual healing that focuses on the power of our thoughts and emotions. The more powerful your thoughts and emotions are, the more likely you are to manifest. By developing the art of focus, you can learn to direct your thoughts and energy to attract more of what you want.

Common Mistakes When Trying to Manifest

There are a few common mistakes people make when they're trying to manifest their desires.

1. Not being specific enough.
One of the most common mistakes people make is not being specific enough about what they want. The more specific you are, the better. The universe needs to know exactly what you want to help you manifest it.

2. Trying to control everything.
Another mistake people make is trying to control everything. When you try to control the manifesting process, you often end up sabotaging yourself.

3. Not taking action.
Another mistake people make is not taking action. Manifestation is a two-way street. You need to take action in order to receive what you want. The universe will provide guidance, but it's up to you to take the necessary steps to achieve your goals.

4. Giving up too soon.
Finally, another common mistake people make is giving up too soon. Manifesting takes time and patience. Don't give up if it doesn't happen immediately. Trust that the universe is working behind the scenes to help you manifest your desires.

If you avoid these common mistakes, you'll be on your way to manifesting your desires.

In summary, prayer, and manifestation are two powerful tools you can use to create the life you want. Use them both to achieve your goals and live the life of your dreams. Just remember to be specific about what you want, take action, and trust that whatever happens is for your highest good.
https://selfpause.com/manifestation/manifestation-vs-prayer

The Methods to Manifestation

The manifesting faith you need to create the life of your dreams is already within you. But to tap into that infinite power, you must be willing to surrender to God's will and timing. This will change the way you think, feel, and speak. Romans 12:2 TPT is foundational for this process.

"Stop imitating the ideals and opinions of the culture around you but be inwardly transformed by the Holy Spirit through a total reformation of how you think. This will empower you to discern God's will as you live a beautiful life, satisfying and perfect in his eyes."
Romans 12:2 TPT

These Methods to Manifesting Your Best Life, will help you take control of your thoughts, beliefs, emotions, and behaviors. This will create a healthy place for you and bring out a wealth of positive emotions while you're manifesting.

- **Release** (negative thoughts and self-talk) Free yourself from the thoughts and inner monologue that speak beneath who God says you are. But trust in the Lord completely and do not rely on your own opinions. *With all your heart, rely on him to guide you, and he will lead you in every decision you make Proverbs 3:5-8 TPT.*

- **Renew** (with affirmations, declarations, and scriptures) *For you have acquired new creation life which is continually being renewed into the likeness of the One who created you.; giving you the full revelation of God Colossians 3:10 TPT.* With a fresh mindset and positive perspective of self, it's time to fill your mind with thoughts, declarations, and scripture that will empower you and prosper you.

- **Re-evaluate** (your situation and yourself) *Examine yourselves, to see whether you are in faith. Test yourselves. Or do you not realize? This about yourselves, that Jesus Christ is in you? Unless indeed you fail to meet the test 2 Corinthians 13:5 ESV.* With a clear mind and new perspective, look at yourself and your situation again; how can you consider these things more constructively now?

- **Rejuvenate** (approach your declarations with new energy and positive feelings) *Let your speech always be generous., seasoned with salt, so that you may know how you ought to answer each person Colossians 4:6 TPT.* Remember that every time you speak an affirming word about yourself, you're speaking LIFE into yourself. Let each word recharge you!

- **Reaffirm** (3-5 times daily) Consistency is important for any habit. Speaking these declarations and reaffirming God's Word multiple times each day also allows them to repeat in your mind. *I will reaffirm my covenant of Blessings to you and your family. I will make sure your descendants are as many as the stars of the heavens. And the grains of sand on the shores. I reaffirm my earlier promises that your descendants will possess the lands and sit in the gates of their enemies, and from your descendants, all the people of the Earth will discover true blessings. All this is because you have obeyed my voice. Genesis 22: 17-19.*

- **Receive** (be ready to receive what you're manifesting; keep your heart and mind open) Though release was the first part of this method, there was still important restructuring that had to happen before you were ready to receive. If in your heart you were still believing the negativity about yourself, unfortunately that's what you'd receive. But now that your mind is clear and you have been spoken into and empowered, your hands are truly free to access the manifested blessings. *Just make sure you ask empowered by confident faith Without doubting that you will receive. For the ambivalent person believes one minute and doubts the next. Being undecided makes you become like the rough seas driven and tossed by the wind you're up one minute and tossed down the next James 1:6 TPT.*

- **Recalibrate** (wherever necessary) As human beings we're not created to be perfect. If at any point you sense a leakage (in mindset etc.) when moving from one step of the method to the next, don't be afraid to go back. This is a marathon not a sprint. Take the time YOU need to progress through. You've got it and God's got you!

What are Your Manifestation Goals

As you become more intentional on manifesting the things you truly desire, it is important to BE CLEAR on WHAT YOU WANT and WRITE IT DOWN.

Ask yourself the following questions before you start.

1. Does it align with my heart beliefs?
2. Do I really want what I am manifesting?
3. Does it add value to my life?
4. Does it align with my purpose, and the season God has me in right now?
5. Does it add to my health?
6. How does it affect those around me?
7. When I think about having it, does it feel right?
8. Does it bring forth generational blessings?
9. Am I ready to receive what I'm manifesting?

Manifestation Goals

DATE	I AM MANIFESTING	MANIFESTED DATE	JOURNAL PAGE #

FAQ About Manifesting

Q: Is using the Law of Attraction while manifesting biblical?

A. People who don't know the history of the law of attraction feel it's a modern concept. And for those who know history, not many are aware of the law of attraction in the Bible. In several verses, the Bible talks about using beliefs, thoughts, and positive thinking feelings to achieve our desire. These are elements upon which manifestation is based. There is biblical evidence that provides clear instructions about the law of attraction, even though it wasn't stated directly in the scripture.[1] (Matthew 9:29, Roman 12:2, Proverbs 23:7, Mark 9:23)

Q: How much time should I spend journaling?

A. Be prepared to take at least 20 minutes in the morning, and 20 minutes at night to use the journal. Every Sunday spend 30 minutes to 1 hour to reflect back on your week to help you keep moving forward.

Q: What if manifesting is not working for me?

A. This challenge will present itself differently to those who experience it, but often it is one's negative thoughts, limiting beliefs, unhealthy emotions, and bad behaviors that is usually the hinderance to one manifesting their best life. The Methods to Manifestation on page 12 will help you feel more positive and healthy emotions while you are manifesting.

Q: Should I create a vision board?

A. Yes! Vision boards are a physical representation of the goals you are manifesting.

Q: Why is writing down my manifestation goals important?

A. It helps to define your goals and intentions and gives you a clear picture of what you want to see manifest.

---

[1] https://manifestlawofattraction.co/law-of-attraction-in-the-bible/

Vision Board Cut-Outs

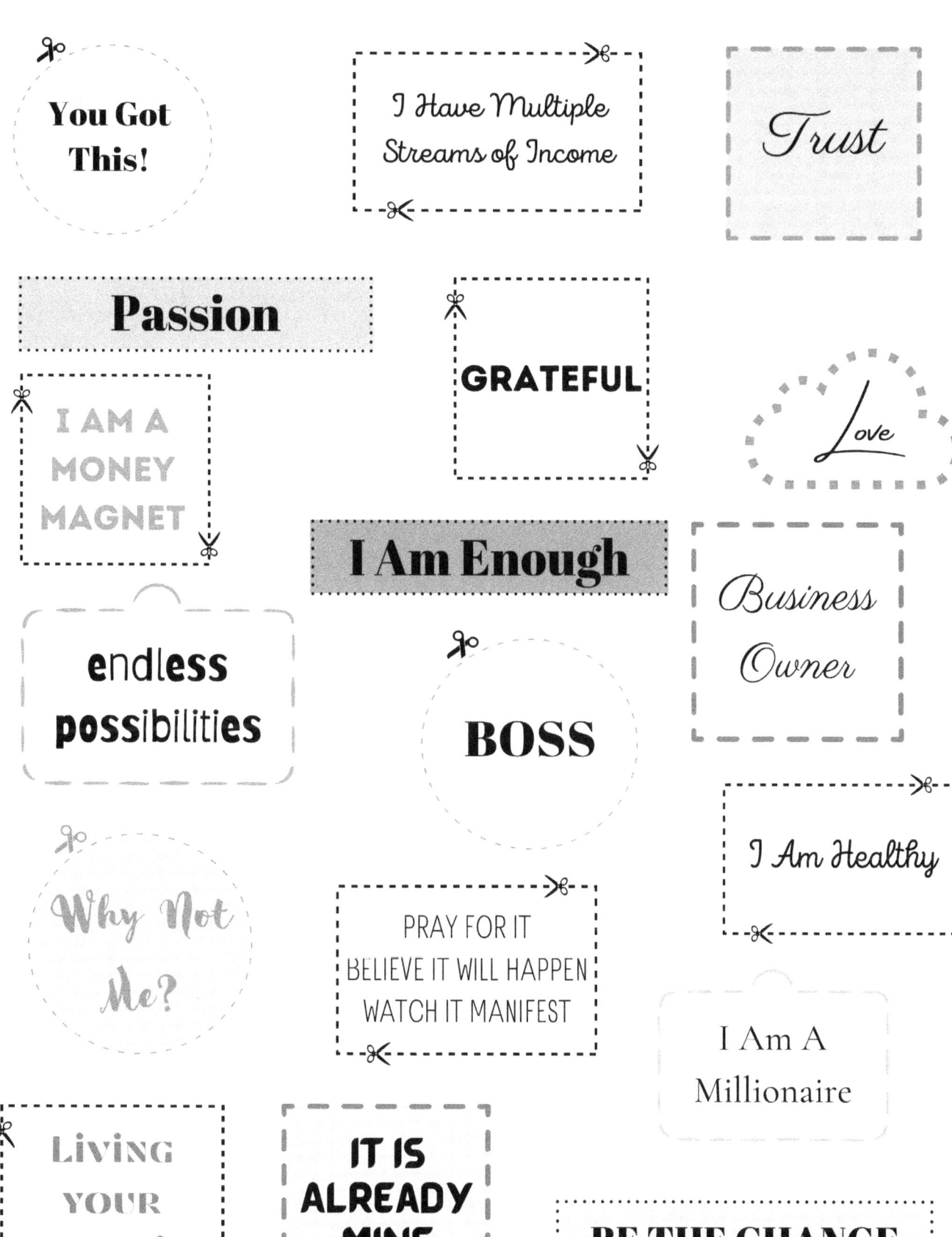

Vision Board-Blank Checks

This page is intentionally blank for your vision board

This page is intentionally blank for your vision board

How to Use This Journal

It's highly encouraged to use this journal during your devotional time. Doing so not only allows you to be intentional about manifesting your best life, but it also allows you to apply God's Word to what you are manifesting. Be prepared to take at least 20 minutes in the morning, and 20 minutes at night to use the journal. Every Sunday, spend 30 minutes to 1 hour to reflect back on your week to help you keep moving forward. Before you start, please find an accountability partner or a community of likeminded people who will be supportive and encourage to stay focused to the end.

"Your life right now is the sum total of every word you've ever spoken in your head and out loud."
- Simon T Bailey

Manifesting Your Best Life

Day: _____   Date: _____

Attitude of Gratitude: What are you thankful for today?

1. _____
2. _____
3. _____
4. _____

Today's Focal Point: What is one thing you are manifesting today?

What Actions will you take to manifest this?

_____
_____
_____
_____

Know Your Why: Why is what you are manifesting special? How will receiving it positively change you?

_____
_____
_____
_____

Your personal Affirmation/Declarations for the day. (Affirm 3-5 times a day)

_____
_____
_____
_____

Manifesting Notes A.M.

Manifesting Notes P.M.

Manifesting Your Best Life

Day: _____   Date: _____

Attitude of Gratitude: What are you thankful for today?

1. _____
2. _____
3. _____
4. _____

Today's Focal Point: What is one thing you are manifesting today?

```
┌─────────────────────────────────────────────────┐
│                                                 │
│                                                 │
│                                                 │
└─────────────────────────────────────────────────┘
```

What Actions will you take to manifest this?

_____
_____
_____
_____

Know Your Why: Why is what you are manifesting special? How will receiving it positively change you?

_____
_____
_____

Your personal Affirmation/Declarations for the day. (Affirm 3-5 times a day)

_____
_____
_____
_____

Manifesting Notes A.M.

Manifesting Notes P.M.

Manifesting Your Best Life

Day: _____   Date: _____

Attitude of Gratitude: What are you thankful for today?

1. _____
2. _____
3. _____
4. _____

Today's Focal Point: What is one thing you are manifesting today?

```
┌─────────────────────────────────────────────────┐
│                                                 │
│                                                 │
│                                                 │
└─────────────────────────────────────────────────┘
```

What Actions will you take to manifest this?

_____
_____
_____
_____

Know Your Why: Why is what you are manifesting special? How will receiving it positively change you?

_____
_____
_____
_____

Your personal Affirmation/Declarations for the day. (Affirm 3-5 times a day)

_____
_____
_____
_____

Manifesting Notes A.M.

Manifesting Notes P.M.

Manifesting Your Best Life

Day: _____   Date: _____

Attitude of Gratitude: What are you thankful for today?

1. _____
2. _____
3. _____
4. _____

Today's Focal Point: What is one thing you are manifesting today?

```
┌─────────────────────────────────────────────────────────┐
│                                                         │
│                                                         │
│                                                         │
└─────────────────────────────────────────────────────────┘
```

What Actions will you take to manifest this?

_____
_____
_____
_____

Know Your Why: Why is what you are manifesting special? How will receiving it positively change you?

_____
_____
_____
_____

Your personal Affirmation/Declarations for the day. (Affirm 3-5 times a day)

_____
_____
_____
_____

Manifesting Notes A.M.

Manifesting Notes P.M.

Manifesting Your Best Life

Day: _____   Date: _____

Attitude of Gratitude: What are you thankful for today?

1. _____
2. _____
3. _____
4. _____

Today's Focal Point: What is one thing you are manifesting today?

[   ]

What Actions will you take to manifest this?

_____
_____
_____
_____

Know Your Why: Why is what you are manifesting special? How will receiving it positively change you?

_____
_____
_____
_____

Your personal Affirmation/Declarations for the day. (Affirm 3-5 times a day)

_____
_____
_____
_____

Manifesting Notes A.M.

_____
_____
_____
_____
_____
_____
_____
_____
_____
_____

Manifesting Notes P.M.

_____
_____
_____
_____
_____
_____
_____
_____
_____
_____

Manifesting Your Best Life

Day: _____   Date: _____

Attitude of Gratitude: What are you thankful for today?

1. _____
2. _____
3. _____
4. _____

Today's Focal Point: What is one thing you are manifesting today?

┌───┐
│   │
│   │
│   │
└───┘

What Actions will you take to manifest this?

_____
_____
_____
_____

Know Your Why: Why is what you are manifesting special? How will receiving it positively change you?

_____
_____
_____

Your personal Affirmation/Declarations for the day. (Affirm 3-5 times a day)

_____
_____
_____
_____

Manifesting Notes A.M.

Manifesting Notes P.M.

Manifesting Your Best Life

Day: _____   Date: _____

Attitude of Gratitude: What are you thankful for today?

1. _____
2. _____
3. _____
4. _____

Today's Focal Point: What is one thing you are manifesting today?

```
┌──────────────────────────────────────────────┐
│                                              │
│                                              │
│                                              │
└──────────────────────────────────────────────┘
```

What Actions will you take to manifest this?

_____
_____
_____
_____

Know Your Why: Why is what you are manifesting special? How will receiving it positively change you?

_____
_____
_____
_____

Your personal Affirmation/Declarations for the day. (Affirm 3-5 times a day)

_____
_____
_____
_____

Manifesting Notes A.M.

Manifesting Notes P.M.

Manifesting Reflections

WEEK 1

Congrats on finishing your first week and applying the attitude of gratitude!

Gratitude Check In: How has gratitude helped you this week?

"Everything you want is out there waiting for you to ask. Everything you want also wants you. But you have to take action to get it."
– Jack Canfield

Manifesting Your Best Life

Day: _____   Date: _____

Attitude of Gratitude: What are you thankful for today?

1. _____
2. _____
3. _____
4. _____

Today's Focal Point: What is one thing you are manifesting today?

```
┌─────────────────────────────────────────────────┐
│                                                 │
│                                                 │
│                                                 │
└─────────────────────────────────────────────────┘
```

What Actions will you take to manifest this?

_____
_____
_____
_____

Know Your Why: Why is what you are manifesting special? How will receiving it positively change you?

_____
_____
_____
_____

Your personal Affirmation/Declarations for the day. (Affirm 3-5 times a day)

_____
_____
_____
_____

Manifesting Notes A.M.

Manifesting Notes P.M.

Manifesting Your Best Life

Day: _____   Date: _____

Attitude of Gratitude: What are you thankful for today?

1. _____
2. _____
3. _____
4. _____

Today's Focal Point: What is one thing you are manifesting today?

```
┌─────────────────────────────────────────────────┐
│                                                 │
│                                                 │
│                                                 │
└─────────────────────────────────────────────────┘
```

What Actions will you take to manifest this?

_____
_____
_____
_____

Know Your Why: Why is what you are manifesting special? How will receiving it positively change you?

_____
_____
_____
_____

Your personal Affirmation/Declarations for the day. (Affirm 3-5 times a day)

_____
_____
_____
_____

Manifesting Notes A.M.

Manifesting Notes P.M.

Manifesting Your Best Life

Day: _____   Date: _____

Attitude of Gratitude: What are you thankful for today?

1. _____
2. _____
3. _____
4. _____

Today's Focal Point: What is one thing you are manifesting today?

```
┌─────────────────────────────────────────────────┐
│                                                 │
│                                                 │
│                                                 │
│                                                 │
└─────────────────────────────────────────────────┘
```

What Actions will you take to manifest this?

_____
_____
_____
_____

Know Your Why: Why is what you are manifesting special? How will receiving it positively change you?

_____
_____
_____
_____

Your personal Affirmation/Declarations for the day. (Affirm 3-5 times a day)

_____
_____
_____

Manifesting Notes A.M.

Manifesting Notes P.M.

Manifesting Your Best Life

Day: _____   Date: _____

Attitude of Gratitude: What are you thankful for today?

1. _____
2. _____
3. _____
4. _____

Today's Focal Point: What is one thing you are manifesting today?

```
┌────────────────────────────────────────────┐
│                                            │
│                                            │
│                                            │
└────────────────────────────────────────────┘
```

What Actions will you take to manifest this?

_____
_____
_____
_____

Know Your Why: Why is what you are manifesting special? How will receiving it positively change you?

_____
_____
_____
_____

Your personal Affirmation/Declarations for the day. (Affirm 3-5 times a day)

_____
_____
_____
_____

Manifesting Notes A.M.

Manifesting Notes P.M.

Manifesting Your Best Life

Day: _____   Date: _____

Attitude of Gratitude: What are you thankful for today?

1. _____
2. _____
3. _____
4. _____

Today's Focal Point: What is one thing you are manifesting today?

```
┌─────────────────────────────────────────────────────────────────┐
│                                                                 │
│                                                                 │
│                                                                 │
└─────────────────────────────────────────────────────────────────┘
```

What Actions will you take to manifest this?

_____
_____
_____
_____

Know Your Why: Why is what you are manifesting special? How will receiving it positively change you?

_____
_____
_____
_____

Your personal Affirmation/Declarations for the day. (Affirm 3-5 times a day)

_____
_____
_____
_____

Manifesting Notes A.M.

Manifesting Notes P.M.

Manifesting Your Best Life

Day: _____   Date: _____

Attitude of Gratitude: What are you thankful for today?

1. _____
2. _____
3. _____
4. _____

Today's Focal Point: What is one thing you are manifesting today?

What Actions will you take to manifest this?

_____
_____
_____
_____

Know Your Why: Why is what you are manifesting special? How will receiving it positively change you?

_____
_____
_____
_____

Your personal Affirmation/Declarations for the day. (Affirm 3-5 times a day)

_____
_____
_____
_____

Manifesting Notes A.M.

Manifesting Notes P.M.

Manifesting Your Best Life

Day: _____   Date: _____

Attitude of Gratitude: What are you thankful for today?

1. _____
2. _____
3. _____
4. _____

Today's Focal Point: What is one thing you are manifesting today?

┌───┐
│   │
│   │
│   │
└───┘

What Actions will you take to manifest this?

_____
_____
_____
_____

Know Your Why: Why is what you are manifesting special? How will receiving it positively change you?

_____
_____
_____
_____

Your personal Affirmation/Declarations for the day. (Affirm 3-5 times a day)

_____
_____
_____
_____

Manifesting Notes A.M.

Manifesting Notes P.M.

Manifesting Reflections

WEEK 2

*Your investment in yourself will be worth it! You deserve to live in ABUNDANCE!
Let's take this next week head on, together!*

How will you invest in yourself next week?

"You will succeed in whatever you choose to do, and light will shine on the road ahead of you."

Job 22:28 NLT

Manifesting Your Best Life

Day: _____   Date: _____

Attitude of Gratitude: What are you thankful for today?

1. _____
2. _____
3. _____
4. _____

Today's Focal Point: What is one thing you are manifesting today?

[   ]

What Actions will you take to manifest this?

_____
_____
_____
_____

Know Your Why: Why is what you are manifesting special? How will receiving it positively change you?

_____
_____
_____
_____

Your personal Affirmation/Declarations for the day. (Affirm 3-5 times a day)

_____
_____
_____
_____

Manifesting Notes A.M.

Manifesting Notes P.M.

Manifesting Your Best Life

Day: _____   Date: _____

Attitude of Gratitude: What are you thankful for today?

1. _____
2. _____
3. _____
4. _____

Today's Focal Point: What is one thing you are manifesting today?

┌──┐
│   │
│   │
│   │
└──┘

What Actions will you take to manifest this?

_____
_____
_____
_____

Know Your Why: Why is what you are manifesting special? How will receiving it positively change you?

_____
_____
_____
_____

Your personal Affirmation/Declarations for the day. (Affirm 3-5 times a day)

_____
_____
_____
_____

Manifesting Notes A.M.

Manifesting Notes P.M.

Manifesting Your Best Life

Day: _____   Date: _____

Attitude of Gratitude: What are you thankful for today?

1. _____
2. _____
3. _____
4. _____

Today's Focal Point: What is one thing you are manifesting today?

```
┌─────────────────────────────────────────────┐
│                                             │
│                                             │
│                                             │
└─────────────────────────────────────────────┘
```

What Actions will you take to manifest this?

_____
_____
_____
_____

Know Your Why: Why is what you are manifesting special? How will receiving it positively change you?

_____
_____
_____
_____

Your personal Affirmation/Declarations for the day. (Affirm 3-5 times a day)

_____
_____
_____

Manifesting Notes A.M.

Manifesting Notes P.M.

Manifesting Your Best Life

Day: _____   Date: _____

Attitude of Gratitude: What are you thankful for today?

1. _____
2. _____
3. _____
4. _____

Today's Focal Point: What is one thing you are manifesting today?

```
┌─────────────────────────────────────────────────┐
│                                                 │
│                                                 │
│                                                 │
└─────────────────────────────────────────────────┘
```

What Actions will you take to manifest this?

_____
_____
_____
_____

Know Your Why: Why is what you are manifesting special? How will receiving it positively change you?

_____
_____
_____
_____

Your personal Affirmation/Declarations for the day. (Affirm 3-5 times a day)

_____
_____
_____
_____

Manifesting Notes A.M.

_____

Manifesting Notes P.M.

Manifesting Your Best Life

Day: _____   Date: _____

Attitude of Gratitude: What are you thankful for today?

1. _____
2. _____
3. _____
4. _____

Today's Focal Point: What is one thing you are manifesting today?

```
┌─────────────────────────────────────────────────────────┐
│                                                         │
│                                                         │
│                                                         │
└─────────────────────────────────────────────────────────┘
```

What Actions will you take to manifest this?

_____
_____
_____
_____

Know Your Why: Why is what you are manifesting special? How will receiving it positively change you?

_____
_____
_____
_____

Your personal Affirmation/Declarations for the day. (Affirm 3-5 times a day)

_____
_____
_____

Manifesting Notes A.M.

Manifesting Notes P.M.

Manifesting Your Best Life

Day: _____   Date: _____

Attitude of Gratitude: What are you thankful for today?

1. _____
2. _____
3. _____
4. _____

Today's Focal Point: What is one thing you are manifesting today?

```
┌─────────────────────────────────────────────────┐
│                                                 │
│                                                 │
│                                                 │
└─────────────────────────────────────────────────┘
```

What Actions will you take to manifest this?

_____
_____
_____
_____

Know Your Why: Why is what you are manifesting special? How will receiving it positively change you?

_____
_____
_____
_____

Your personal Affirmation/Declarations for the day. (Affirm 3-5 times a day)

_____
_____
_____
_____

Manifesting Notes A.M.

Manifesting Notes P.M.

Manifesting Your Best Life

Day: _____   Date: _____

Attitude of Gratitude: What are you thankful for today?

1. _____
2. _____
3. _____
4. _____

Today's Focal Point: What is one thing you are manifesting today?

What Actions will you take to manifest this?

_____
_____
_____
_____

Know Your Why: Why is what you are manifesting special? How will receiving it positively change you?

_____
_____
_____
_____

Your personal Affirmation/Declarations for the day. (Affirm 3-5 times a day)

_____
_____
_____
_____

Manifesting Notes A.M.

Manifesting Notes P.M.

Manifesting Reflections

WEEK 3

Look at you go! As you move forward, your thought patterns begin to change with consistency.

How are you feeling so far on this manifesting journey?

"It's our intention. Our intention is everything. Nothing happens on this planet without it. Not one single thing has ever been accomplished without intention."
– Jim Carrey

Manifesting Your Best Life

Day: _____   Date: _____

Attitude of Gratitude: What are you thankful for today?

1. _____
2. _____
3. _____
4. _____

Today's Focal Point: What is one thing you are manifesting today?

[   ]

What Actions will you take to manifest this?

_____
_____
_____
_____

Know Your Why: Why is what you are manifesting special? How will receiving it positively change you?

_____
_____
_____
_____

Your personal Affirmation/Declarations for the day. (Affirm 3-5 times a day)

_____
_____
_____
_____

Manifesting Notes A.M.

Manifesting Notes P.M.

Manifesting Your Best Life

Day: _____   Date: _____

Attitude of Gratitude: What are you thankful for today?

1. _____
2. _____
3. _____
4. _____

Today's Focal Point: What is one thing you are manifesting today?

```
┌─────────────────────────────────────────────────────────┐
│                                                         │
│                                                         │
│                                                         │
│                                                         │
└─────────────────────────────────────────────────────────┘
```

What Actions will you take to manifest this?

_____
_____
_____
_____

Know Your Why: Why is what you are manifesting special? How will receiving it positively change you?

_____
_____
_____
_____

Your personal Affirmation/Declarations for the day. (Affirm 3-5 times a day)

_____
_____
_____
_____

Manifesting Notes A.M.

Manifesting Notes P.M.

Manifesting Your Best Life

Day: _____   Date: _____

Attitude of Gratitude: What are you thankful for today?

1. _____
2. _____
3. _____
4. _____

Today's Focal Point: What is one thing you are manifesting today?

┌───┐
│   │
│   │
│   │
└───┘

What Actions will you take to manifest this?

_____
_____
_____
_____

Know Your Why: Why is what you are manifesting special? How will receiving it positively change you?

_____
_____
_____
_____

Your personal Affirmation/Declarations for the day. (Affirm 3-5 times a day)

_____
_____
_____
_____

Manifesting Notes A.M.

Manifesting Notes P.M.

Manifesting Your Best Life

Day: _____   Date: _____

Attitude of Gratitude: What are you thankful for today?

1. _____
2. _____
3. _____
4. _____

Today's Focal Point: What is one thing you are manifesting today?

[   ]

What Actions will you take to manifest this?

_____
_____
_____
_____

Know Your Why: Why is what you are manifesting special? How will receiving it positively change you?

_____
_____
_____
_____

Your personal Affirmation/Declarations for the day. (Affirm 3-5 times a day)

_____
_____
_____
_____

Manifesting Notes A.M.

Manifesting Notes P.M.

Manifesting Your Best Life

Day: _____   Date: _____

Attitude of Gratitude: What are you thankful for today?

1. _____
2. _____
3. _____
4. _____

Today's Focal Point: What is one thing you are manifesting today?

┌───┐
│   │
│   │
│   │
└───┘

What Actions will you take to manifest this?

_____
_____
_____
_____

Know Your Why: Why is what you are manifesting special? How will receiving it positively change you?

_____
_____
_____
_____

Your personal Affirmation/Declarations for the day. (Affirm 3-5 times a day)

_____
_____
_____
_____

Manifesting Notes A.M.

Manifesting Notes P.M.

Manifesting Your Best Life

Day: _____   Date: _____

Attitude of Gratitude: What are you thankful for today?

1. _____
2. _____
3. _____
4. _____

Today's Focal Point: What is one thing you are manifesting today?

```
┌─                                                      ─┐



└─                                                      ─┘
```

What Actions will you take to manifest this?

_____
_____
_____
_____

Know Your Why: Why is what you are manifesting special? How will receiving it positively change you?

_____
_____
_____
_____

Your personal Affirmation/Declarations for the day. (Affirm 3-5 times a day)

_____
_____
_____
_____

Manifesting Notes A.M.

Manifesting Notes P.M.

Manifesting Your Best Life

Day: _____   Date: _____

Attitude of Gratitude: What are you thankful for today?

1. _____
2. _____
3. _____
4. _____

Today's Focal Point: What is one thing you are manifesting today?

```
┌──────────────────────────────────────────────┐
│                                              │
│                                              │
│                                              │
└──────────────────────────────────────────────┘
```

What Actions will you take to manifest this?

_____
_____
_____
_____

Know Your Why: Why is what you are manifesting special? How will receiving it positively change you?

_____
_____
_____
_____

Your personal Affirmation/Declarations for the day. (Affirm 3-5 times a day)

_____
_____
_____
_____

Manifesting Notes A.M.

Manifesting Notes P.M.

Manifesting Reflections

WEEK 4

Stay committed! Thank you for inviting us on this journey of transformation with you!

What was you inspiration this week?

"Your whole life is a manifestation of the thoughts that go on in your head."
– Lisa Nichols

Manifesting Your Best Life

Day: _____   Date: _____

Attitude of Gratitude: What are you thankful for today?

1. _____
2. _____
3. _____
4. _____

Today's Focal Point: What is one thing you are manifesting today?

┌───┐
│   │
│   │
│   │
└───┘

What Actions will you take to manifest this?

_____
_____
_____
_____

Know Your Why: Why is what you are manifesting special? How will receiving it positively change you?

_____
_____
_____
_____

Your personal Affirmation/Declarations for the day. (Affirm 3-5 times a day)

_____
_____
_____
_____

Manifesting Notes A.M.

Manifesting Notes P.M.

Manifesting Your Best Life

Day: _____   Date: _____

Attitude of Gratitude: What are you thankful for today?

1. _____
2. _____
3. _____
4. _____

Today's Focal Point: What is one thing you are manifesting today?

````



````

What Actions will you take to manifest this?

_____
_____
_____
_____

Know Your Why: Why is what you are manifesting special? How will receiving it positively change you?

_____
_____
_____
_____

Your personal Affirmation/Declarations for the day. (Affirm 3-5 times a day)

_____
_____
_____
_____

Manifesting Notes A.M.

Manifesting Notes P.M.

Manifesting Your Best Life

Day: _____   Date: _____

Attitude of Gratitude: What are you thankful for today?

1. _____
2. _____
3. _____
4. _____

Today's Focal Point: What is one thing you are manifesting today?

⌐───┐
│   │
│   │
│   │
└───┘

What Actions will you take to manifest this?

_____
_____
_____
_____

Know Your Why: Why is what you are manifesting special? How will receiving it positively change you?

_____
_____
_____

Your personal Affirmation/Declarations for the day. (Affirm 3-5 times a day)

_____
_____
_____

Manifesting Notes A.M.

Manifesting Notes P.M.

Manifesting Your Best Life

Day: _____   Date: _____

Attitude of Gratitude: What are you thankful for today?

1. _____
2. _____
3. _____
4. _____

Today's Focal Point: What is one thing you are manifesting today?

┌───┐
│   │
│   │
│   │
└───┘

What Actions will you take to manifest this?

_____
_____
_____
_____

Know Your Why: Why is what you are manifesting special? How will receiving it positively change you?

_____
_____
_____
_____

Your personal Affirmation/Declarations for the day. (Affirm 3-5 times a day)

_____
_____
_____

Manifesting Notes A.M.

Manifesting Notes P.M.

Manifesting Your Best Life

Day: _____   Date: _____

Attitude of Gratitude: What are you thankful for today?

1. _____
2. _____
3. _____
4. _____

Today's Focal Point: What is one thing you are manifesting today?

[   ]

What Actions will you take to manifest this?

_____
_____
_____
_____

Know Your Why: Why is what you are manifesting special? How will receiving it positively change you?

_____
_____
_____
_____

Your personal Affirmation/Declarations for the day. (Affirm 3-5 times a day)

_____
_____
_____
_____

Manifesting Notes A.M.

Manifesting Notes P.M.

Manifesting Your Best Life

Day: _____   Date: _____

Attitude of Gratitude: What are you thankful for today?

1. _____
2. _____
3. _____
4. _____

Today's Focal Point: What is one thing you are manifesting today?

[   ]

What Actions will you take to manifest this?

_____
_____
_____
_____

Know Your Why: Why is what you are manifesting special? How will receiving it positively change you?

_____
_____
_____
_____

Your personal Affirmation/Declarations for the day. (Affirm 3-5 times a day)

_____
_____
_____
_____

Manifesting Notes A.M.

Manifesting Notes P.M.

Manifesting Your Best Life

Day: _____   Date: _____

Attitude of Gratitude: What are you thankful for today?

1. _____
2. _____
3. _____
4. _____

Today's Focal Point: What is one thing you are manifesting today?

┌──┐
│   │
│   │
│   │
└──┘

What Actions will you take to manifest this?

_____
_____
_____
_____

Know Your Why: Why is what you are manifesting special? How will receiving it positively change you?

_____
_____
_____
_____

Your personal Affirmation/Declarations for the day. (Affirm 3-5 times a day)

_____
_____
_____
_____

Manifesting Notes A.M.

Manifesting Notes P.M.

Manifesting Reflections

WEEK 5

Along with gratitude, remember to show yourself grace during this process.
It isn't easy manifesting your wildest dreams!

Grace

How will you show yourself grace next week?

"Your words are so powerful that they will kill or give life, and the talkative person will reap the consequences."
Proverbs 18:21 TPT

Manifesting Your Best Life

Day: _____   Date: _____

Attitude of Gratitude: What are you thankful for today?

1. _____
2. _____
3. _____
4. _____

Today's Focal Point: What is one thing you are manifesting today?

```
┌─────────────────────────────────────────────────┐
│                                                 │
│                                                 │
│                                                 │
└─────────────────────────────────────────────────┘
```

What Actions will you take to manifest this?

_____
_____
_____
_____

Know Your Why: Why is what you are manifesting special? How will receiving it positively change you?

_____
_____
_____
_____

Your personal Affirmation/Declarations for the day. (Affirm 3-5 times a day)

_____
_____
_____
_____

Manifesting Notes A.M.

Manifesting Notes P.M.

Manifesting Your Best Life

Day: _____   Date: _____

Attitude of Gratitude: What are you thankful for today?

1. _____
2. _____
3. _____
4. _____

Today's Focal Point: What is one thing you are manifesting today?

```
┌─────────────────────────────────────────────────────────┐
│                                                         │
│                                                         │
│                                                         │
│                                                         │
└─────────────────────────────────────────────────────────┘
```

What Actions will you take to manifest this?

_____
_____
_____
_____

Know Your Why: Why is what you are manifesting special? How will receiving it positively change you?

_____
_____
_____
_____

Your personal Affirmation/Declarations for the day. (Affirm 3-5 times a day)

_____
_____
_____
_____

Manifesting Notes A.M.

Manifesting Notes P.M.

Manifesting Your Best Life

Day: _____   Date: _____

Attitude of Gratitude: What are you thankful for today?

1. _____
2. _____
3. _____
4. _____

Today's Focal Point: What is one thing you are manifesting today?

```
┌─────────────────────────────────────────────────────────────────┐
│                                                                 │
│                                                                 │
│                                                                 │
│                                                                 │
└─────────────────────────────────────────────────────────────────┘
```

What Actions will you take to manifest this?

_____
_____
_____
_____

Know Your Why: Why is what you are manifesting special? How will receiving it positively change you?

_____
_____
_____
_____

Your personal Affirmation/Declarations for the day. (Affirm 3-5 times a day)

_____
_____
_____
_____

Manifesting Notes A.M.

Manifesting Notes P.M.

Manifesting Your Best Life

Day: _____   Date: _____

Attitude of Gratitude: What are you thankful for today?

1. _____
2. _____
3. _____
4. _____

Today's Focal Point: What is one thing you are manifesting today?

```
┌─────────────────────────────────────────────────┐
│                                                 │
│                                                 │
│                                                 │
│                                                 │
└─────────────────────────────────────────────────┘
```

What Actions will you take to manifest this?

_____
_____
_____
_____

Know Your Why: Why is what you are manifesting special? How will receiving it positively change you?

_____
_____
_____
_____

Your personal Affirmation/Declarations for the day. (Affirm 3-5 times a day)

_____
_____
_____
_____

Manifesting Notes A.M.

Manifesting Notes P.M.

Manifesting Your Best Life

Day: _____   Date: _____

Attitude of Gratitude: What are you thankful for today?

1. _____
2. _____
3. _____
4. _____

Today's Focal Point: What is one thing you are manifesting today?

```
┌─────────────────────────────────────────────────┐
│                                                 │
│                                                 │
│                                                 │
└─────────────────────────────────────────────────┘
```

What Actions will you take to manifest this?

_____
_____
_____
_____

Know Your Why: Why is what you are manifesting special? How will receiving it positively change you?

_____
_____
_____
_____

Your personal Affirmation/Declarations for the day. (Affirm 3-5 times a day)

_____
_____
_____
_____

Manifesting Notes A.M.

_____
_____
_____
_____
_____
_____
_____
_____
_____
_____

Manifesting Notes P.M.

_____
_____
_____
_____
_____
_____
_____
_____
_____
_____
_____

Manifesting Your Best Life

Day: _____   Date: _____

Attitude of Gratitude: What are you thankful for today?

1. _____
2. _____
3. _____
4. _____

Today's Focal Point: What is one thing you are manifesting today?

```
┌─────────────────────────────────────────────────┐
│                                                 │
│                                                 │
│                                                 │
└─────────────────────────────────────────────────┘
```

What Actions will you take to manifest this?

_____
_____
_____
_____

Know Your Why: Why is what you are manifesting special? How will receiving it positively change you?

_____
_____
_____
_____

Your personal Affirmation/Declarations for the day. (Affirm 3-5 times a day)

_____
_____
_____

Manifesting Notes A.M.

_____
_____
_____
_____
_____
_____
_____
_____
_____

Manifesting Notes P.M.

_____
_____
_____
_____
_____
_____
_____
_____
_____
_____
_____

Manifesting Your Best Life

Day: _____   Date: _____

Attitude of Gratitude: What are you thankful for today?

1. _____
2. _____
3. _____
4. _____

Today's Focal Point: What is one thing you are manifesting today?

```
┌─────────────────────────────────────────────────────────────┐
│                                                             │
│                                                             │
│                                                             │
└─────────────────────────────────────────────────────────────┘
```

What Actions will you take to manifest this?

_____
_____
_____
_____

Know Your Why: Why is what you are manifesting special? How will receiving it positively change you?

_____
_____
_____
_____

Your personal Affirmation/Declarations for the day. (Affirm 3-5 times a day)

_____
_____
_____
_____

Manifesting Notes A.M.

Manifesting Notes P.M.

Manifesting Reflections

WEEK 6

Have faith! Continue to dream! Keep on believing!

What can you do to make yourself feel empowered for next week?

"Keep your thoughts positive because your thoughts become your words. Keep your words positive because your words become your behavior. Keep your behavior positive because your behavior becomes your habits. Keep your habits positive because your habits become your values. Keep your values positive because your values become your destiny."

– Gandhi

Manifesting Your Best Life

Day: _____   Date: _____

Attitude of Gratitude: What are you thankful for today?

1. _____
2. _____
3. _____
4. _____

Today's Focal Point: What is one thing you are manifesting today?

```
┌─────────────────────────────────────────────────┐
│                                                 │
│                                                 │
│                                                 │
└─────────────────────────────────────────────────┘
```

What Actions will you take to manifest this?

_____
_____
_____
_____

Know Your Why: Why is what you are manifesting special? How will receiving it positively change you?

_____
_____
_____
_____

Your personal Affirmation/Declarations for the day. (Affirm 3-5 times a day)

_____
_____
_____
_____

Manifesting Notes A.M.

Manifesting Notes P.M.

Manifesting Your Best Life

Day: _____   Date: _____

Attitude of Gratitude: What are you thankful for today?

1. _____
2. _____
3. _____
4. _____

Today's Focal Point: What is one thing you are manifesting today?

```
┌─────────────────────────────────────────────────┐
│                                                 │
│                                                 │
│                                                 │
└─────────────────────────────────────────────────┘
```

What Actions will you take to manifest this?

_____
_____
_____
_____

Know Your Why: Why is what you are manifesting special? How will receiving it positively change you?

_____
_____
_____
_____

Your personal Affirmation/Declarations for the day. (Affirm 3-5 times a day)

_____
_____
_____
_____

Manifesting Notes A.M.

Manifesting Notes P.M.

Manifesting Your Best Life

Day: _____   Date: _____

Attitude of Gratitude: What are you thankful for today?

1. _____
2. _____
3. _____
4. _____

Today's Focal Point: What is one thing you are manifesting today?

```
┌─────────────────────────────────────────────┐
│                                             │
│                                             │
│                                             │
└─────────────────────────────────────────────┘
```

What Actions will you take to manifest this?

_____
_____
_____
_____

Know Your Why: Why is what you are manifesting special? How will receiving it positively change you?

_____
_____
_____
_____

Your personal Affirmation/Declarations for the day. (Affirm 3-5 times a day)

_____
_____
_____
_____

Manifesting Notes A.M.

Manifesting Notes P.M.

Manifesting Your Best Life

Day: _____   Date: _____

Attitude of Gratitude: What are you thankful for today?

1. _____
2. _____
3. _____
4. _____

Today's Focal Point: What is one thing you are manifesting today?

[   ]

What Actions will you take to manifest this?

_____
_____
_____
_____

Know Your Why: Why is what you are manifesting special? How will receiving it positively change you?

_____
_____
_____
_____

Your personal Affirmation/Declarations for the day. (Affirm 3-5 times a day)

_____
_____
_____
_____

Manifesting Notes A.M.

Manifesting Notes P.M.

Manifesting Your Best Life

Day: _____ Date: _____

Attitude of Gratitude: What are you thankful for today?

1. _____
2. _____
3. _____
4. _____

Today's Focal Point: What is one thing you are manifesting today?

```
┌─────────────────────────────────────────────────┐
│                                                 │
│                                                 │
│                                                 │
└─────────────────────────────────────────────────┘
```

What Actions will you take to manifest this?

_____
_____
_____
_____

Know Your Why: Why is what you are manifesting special? How will receiving it positively change you?

_____
_____
_____
_____

Your personal Affirmation/Declarations for the day. (Affirm 3-5 times a day)

_____
_____
_____
_____

Manifesting Notes A.M.

Manifesting Notes P.M.

Manifesting Your Best Life

Day: _____   Date: _____

Attitude of Gratitude: What are you thankful for today?

1. _____
2. _____
3. _____
4. _____

Today's Focal Point: What is one thing you are manifesting today?

```
┌─────────────────────────────────────────────────┐
│                                                 │
│                                                 │
│                                                 │
└─────────────────────────────────────────────────┘
```

What Actions will you take to manifest this?

_____
_____
_____
_____

Know Your Why: Why is what you are manifesting special? How will receiving it positively change you?

_____
_____
_____
_____

Your personal Affirmation/Declarations for the day. (Affirm 3-5 times a day)

_____
_____
_____
_____

Manifesting Notes A.M.

Manifesting Notes P.M.

Manifesting Your Best Life

Day: _____   Date: _____

Attitude of Gratitude: What are you thankful for today?

1. _____
2. _____
3. _____
4. _____

Today's Focal Point: What is one thing you are manifesting today?

[   ]

What Actions will you take to manifest this?

_____
_____
_____
_____

Know Your Why: Why is what you are manifesting special? How will receiving it positively change you?

_____
_____
_____
_____

Your personal Affirmation/Declarations for the day. (Affirm 3-5 times a day)

_____
_____
_____
_____

Manifesting Notes A.M.

Manifesting Notes P.M.

Manifesting Reflections

WEEK 7

How you talk to yourself outside of your manifest journal is just as important as how you write about yourself within it. Write Out Your Positive Self-Talk!

Write down 5 Amazing Things about yourself!

"You manifest what you believe, not what you want."
– Sonia Ricotti

Manifesting Your Best Life

Day: _____   Date: _____

Attitude of Gratitude: What are you thankful for today?

1. _____
2. _____
3. _____
4. _____

Today's Focal Point: What is one thing you are manifesting today?

```
┌─────────────────────────────────────────────────────────┐
│                                                         │
│                                                         │
│                                                         │
└─────────────────────────────────────────────────────────┘
```

What Actions will you take to manifest this?

_____
_____
_____
_____

Know Your Why: Why is what you are manifesting special? How will receiving it positively change you?

_____
_____
_____
_____

Your personal Affirmation/Declarations for the day. (Affirm 3-5 times a day)

_____
_____
_____
_____

Manifesting Notes A.M.

Manifesting Notes P.M.

Manifesting Your Best Life

Day: _____ Date: _____

Attitude of Gratitude: What are you thankful for today?

1. _____
2. _____
3. _____
4. _____

Today's Focal Point: What is one thing you are manifesting today?

```
┌──────────────────────────────────────────────────┐
│                                                  │
│                                                  │
│                                                  │
└──────────────────────────────────────────────────┘
```

What Actions will you take to manifest this?

_____
_____
_____
_____

Know Your Why: Why is what you are manifesting special? How will receiving it positively change you?

_____
_____
_____
_____

Your personal Affirmation/Declarations for the day. (Affirm 3-5 times a day)

_____
_____
_____
_____

Manifesting Notes A.M.

Manifesting Notes P.M.

Manifesting Your Best Life

Day: _____   Date: _____

Attitude of Gratitude: What are you thankful for today?

1. _____
2. _____
3. _____
4. _____

Today's Focal Point: What is one thing you are manifesting today?

```
┌─────────────────────────────────────────────────┐
│                                                 │
│                                                 │
│                                                 │
└─────────────────────────────────────────────────┘
```

What Actions will you take to manifest this?

_____
_____
_____
_____

Know Your Why: Why is what you are manifesting special? How will receiving it positively change you?

_____
_____
_____
_____

Your personal Affirmation/Declarations for the day. (Affirm 3-5 times a day)

_____
_____
_____
_____

Manifesting Notes A.M.

Manifesting Notes P.M.

Manifesting Your Best Life

Day: _____   Date: _____

Attitude of Gratitude: What are you thankful for today?

1. _____
2. _____
3. _____
4. _____

Today's Focal Point: What is one thing you are manifesting today?

```
┌─────────────────────────────────────────────────┐
│                                                 │
│                                                 │
│                                                 │
└─────────────────────────────────────────────────┘
```

What Actions will you take to manifest this?

_____
_____
_____
_____

Know Your Why: Why is what you are manifesting special? How will receiving it positively change you?

_____
_____
_____

Your personal Affirmation/Declarations for the day. (Affirm 3-5 times a day)

_____
_____
_____
_____

Manifesting Notes A.M.

Manifesting Notes P.M.

Manifesting Your Best Life

Day: _____   Date: _____

Attitude of Gratitude: What are you thankful for today?

1. _____
2. _____
3. _____
4. _____

Today's Focal Point: What is one thing you are manifesting today?

```
┌─────────────────────────────────────────────────┐
│                                                 │
│                                                 │
│                                                 │
└─────────────────────────────────────────────────┘
```

What Actions will you take to manifest this?

_____
_____
_____
_____

Know Your Why: Why is what you are manifesting special? How will receiving it positively change you?

_____
_____
_____
_____

Your personal Affirmation/Declarations for the day. (Affirm 3-5 times a day)

_____
_____
_____
_____

Manifesting Notes A.M.

Manifesting Notes P.M.

Manifesting Your Best Life

Day: _____   Date: _____

Attitude of Gratitude: What are you thankful for today?

1. _____
2. _____
3. _____
4. _____

Today's Focal Point: What is one thing you are manifesting today?

┌───┐
│   │
│   │
│   │
└───┘

What Actions will you take to manifest this?

_____
_____
_____
_____

Know Your Why: Why is what you are manifesting special? How will receiving it positively change you?

_____
_____
_____
_____

Your personal Affirmation/Declarations for the day. (Affirm 3-5 times a day)

_____
_____
_____
_____

Manifesting Notes A.M.

Manifesting Notes P.M.

Manifesting Your Best Life

Day: _____   Date: _____

Attitude of Gratitude: What are you thankful for today?

1. _____
2. _____
3. _____
4. _____

Today's Focal Point: What is one thing you are manifesting today?

┌───┐
│   │
│   │
│   │
└───┘

What Actions will you take to manifest this?

_____
_____
_____
_____

Know Your Why: Why is what you are manifesting special? How will receiving it positively change you?

_____
_____
_____
_____

Your personal Affirmation/Declarations for the day. (Affirm 3-5 times a day)

_____
_____
_____
_____

Manifesting Notes A.M.

Manifesting Notes P.M.

Manifesting Reflections

WEEK 8

It's been said that words create worlds so let your affirmations lead you into new beginnings! It's only upward from here!

LIVE -your- DREAM

Write fun and positive affirmation for next week and share it with a friend!

"Think the thought until you believe it, and once you believe it, it is."
-Abraham Hicks

Manifesting Your Best Life

Day: _____   Date: _____

Attitude of Gratitude: What are you thankful for today?

1. _____
2. _____
3. _____
4. _____

Today's Focal Point: What is one thing you are manifesting today?

[   ]

What Actions will you take to manifest this?

_____
_____
_____
_____

Know Your Why: Why is what you are manifesting special? How will receiving it positively change you?

_____
_____
_____
_____

Your personal Affirmation/Declarations for the day. (Affirm 3-5 times a day)

_____
_____
_____

Manifesting Notes A.M.

Manifesting Notes P.M.

Manifesting Your Best Life

Day: _____   Date: _____

Attitude of Gratitude: What are you thankful for today?

1. _____
2. _____
3. _____
4. _____

Today's Focal Point: What is one thing you are manifesting today?

```
┌─────────────────────────────────────────────────────────┐
│                                                         │
│                                                         │
│                                                         │
└─────────────────────────────────────────────────────────┘
```

What Actions will you take to manifest this?

_____
_____
_____
_____

Know Your Why: Why is what you are manifesting special? How will receiving it positively change you?

_____
_____
_____
_____

Your personal Affirmation/Declarations for the day. (Affirm 3-5 times a day)

_____
_____
_____
_____

Manifesting Notes A.M.

Manifesting Notes P.M.

Manifesting Your Best Life

Day: _____   Date: _____

Attitude of Gratitude: What are you thankful for today?

1. _____
2. _____
3. _____
4. _____

Today's Focal Point: What is one thing you are manifesting today?

What Actions will you take to manifest this?

_____
_____
_____
_____

Know Your Why: Why is what you are manifesting special? How will receiving it positively change you?

_____
_____
_____
_____

Your personal Affirmation/Declarations for the day. (Affirm 3-5 times a day)

_____
_____
_____
_____

Manifesting Notes A.M.

Manifesting Notes P.M.

Manifesting Your Best Life

Day: _____   Date: _____

Attitude of Gratitude: What are you thankful for today?

1. _____
2. _____
3. _____
4. _____

Today's Focal Point: What is one thing you are manifesting today?

```
┌─────────────────────────────────────────────────┐
│                                                 │
│                                                 │
│                                                 │
└─────────────────────────────────────────────────┘
```

What Actions will you take to manifest this?

_____
_____
_____
_____

Know Your Why: Why is what you are manifesting special? How will receiving it positively change you?

_____
_____
_____
_____

Your personal Affirmation/Declarations for the day. (Affirm 3-5 times a day)

_____
_____
_____
_____

Manifesting Notes A.M.

Manifesting Notes P.M.

Manifesting Your Best Life

Day: _____   Date: _____

Attitude of Gratitude: What are you thankful for today?

1. _____
2. _____
3. _____
4. _____

Today's Focal Point: What is one thing you are manifesting today?

[   ]

What Actions will you take to manifest this?

_____
_____
_____
_____

Know Your Why: Why is what you are manifesting special? How will receiving it positively change you?

_____
_____
_____
_____

Your personal Affirmation/Declarations for the day. (Affirm 3-5 times a day)

_____
_____
_____
_____

Manifesting Notes A.M.

Manifesting Notes P.M.

Manifesting Your Best Life

Day: _____   Date: _____

Attitude of Gratitude: What are you thankful for today?

1. _____
2. _____
3. _____
4. _____

Today's Focal Point: What is one thing you are manifesting today?

```
┌─────────────────────────────────────────────────────────┐
│                                                         │
│                                                         │
│                                                         │
└─────────────────────────────────────────────────────────┘
```

What Actions will you take to manifest this?

_____
_____
_____
_____

Know Your Why: Why is what you are manifesting special? How will receiving it positively change you?

_____
_____
_____
_____

Your personal Affirmation/Declarations for the day. (Affirm 3-5 times a day)

_____
_____
_____
_____

Manifesting Notes A.M.

Manifesting Notes P.M.

Manifesting Your Best Life

Day: _____   Date: _____

Attitude of Gratitude: What are you thankful for today?

1. _____
2. _____
3. _____
4. _____

Today's Focal Point: What is one thing you are manifesting today?

[   ]

What Actions will you take to manifest this?

_____
_____
_____
_____

Know Your Why: Why is what you are manifesting special? How will receiving it positively change you?

_____
_____
_____
_____

Your personal Affirmation/Declarations for the day. (Affirm 3-5 times a day)

_____
_____
_____
_____

Manifesting Notes A.M.

Manifesting Notes P.M.

Manifesting Reflections

WEEK 9

All that you're hoping for, believe you have received it! All you've been waiting for, claim it because it's yours RIGHT NOW!

What is your personal definition of abundance?

"Beloved friend, I pray that you are prospering in every way and that you continually enjoy good health, just as your soul is prospering."
3 John 2 TPT

Manifesting Your Best Life

Day: _____   Date: _____

Attitude of Gratitude: What are you thankful for today?

1. _____
2. _____
3. _____
4. _____

Today's Focal Point: What is one thing you are manifesting today?

```
┌─────────────────────────────────────────────────┐
│                                                 │
│                                                 │
│                                                 │
└─────────────────────────────────────────────────┘
```

What Actions will you take to manifest this?

_____
_____
_____
_____

Know Your Why: Why is what you are manifesting special? How will receiving it positively change you?

_____
_____
_____
_____

Your personal Affirmation/Declarations for the day. (Affirm 3-5 times a day)

_____
_____
_____
_____

Manifesting Notes A.M.

Manifesting Notes P.M.

Manifesting Your Best Life

Day: _____   Date: _____

Attitude of Gratitude: What are you thankful for today?

1. _____
2. _____
3. _____
4. _____

Today's Focal Point: What is one thing you are manifesting today?

```
┌─                                                              ─┐

│                                                                │

└─                                                              ─┘
```

What Actions will you take to manifest this?

_____
_____
_____
_____

Know Your Why: Why is what you are manifesting special? How will receiving it positively change you?

_____
_____
_____
_____

Your personal Affirmation/Declarations for the day. (Affirm 3-5 times a day)

_____
_____
_____
_____

Manifesting Notes A.M.

Manifesting Notes P.M.

Manifesting Your Best Life

Day: _____   Date: _____

Attitude of Gratitude: What are you thankful for today?

1. _____
2. _____
3. _____
4. _____

Today's Focal Point: What is one thing you are manifesting today?

┌───┐
│   │
│   │
│   │
└───┘

What Actions will you take to manifest this?

_____
_____
_____
_____

Know Your Why: Why is what you are manifesting special? How will receiving it positively change you?

_____
_____
_____
_____

Your personal Affirmation/Declarations for the day. (Affirm 3-5 times a day)

_____
_____
_____
_____

Manifesting Notes A.M.

Manifesting Notes P.M.

Manifesting Your Best Life

Day: _____   Date: _____

Attitude of Gratitude: What are you thankful for today?

1. _____
2. _____
3. _____
4. _____

Today's Focal Point: What is one thing you are manifesting today?

┌───┐
│   │
│   │
│   │
└───┘

What Actions will you take to manifest this?

_____
_____
_____
_____

Know Your Why: Why is what you are manifesting special? How will receiving it positively change you?

_____
_____
_____
_____

Your personal Affirmation/Declarations for the day. (Affirm 3-5 times a day)

_____
_____
_____
_____

Manifesting Notes A.M.

_____
_____
_____
_____
_____
_____
_____
_____
_____
_____

Manifesting Notes P.M.

_____
_____
_____
_____
_____
_____
_____
_____
_____
_____

Manifesting Your Best Life

Day: _____   Date: _____

Attitude of Gratitude: What are you thankful for today?

1. _____
2. _____
3. _____
4. _____

Today's Focal Point: What is one thing you are manifesting today?

┌───┐
│   │
│   │
│   │
└───┘

What Actions will you take to manifest this?

_____
_____
_____
_____

Know Your Why: Why is what you are manifesting special? How will receiving it positively change you?

_____
_____
_____
_____

Your personal Affirmation/Declarations for the day. (Affirm 3-5 times a day)

_____
_____
_____
_____

Manifesting Notes A.M.

Manifesting Notes P.M.

Manifesting Your Best Life

Day: _____   Date: _____

Attitude of Gratitude: What are you thankful for today?

1. _____
2. _____
3. _____
4. _____

Today's Focal Point: What is one thing you are manifesting today?

```
┌─────────────────────────────────────────────────┐
│                                                 │
│                                                 │
│                                                 │
└─────────────────────────────────────────────────┘
```

What Actions will you take to manifest this?

_____
_____
_____
_____

Know Your Why: Why is what you are manifesting special? How will receiving it positively change you?

_____
_____
_____
_____

Your personal Affirmation/Declarations for the day. (Affirm 3-5 times a day)

_____
_____
_____
_____

Manifesting Notes A.M.

Manifesting Notes P.M.

Manifesting Your Best Life

Day: _____   Date: _____

Attitude of Gratitude: What are you thankful for today?

1. _____
2. _____
3. _____
4. _____

Today's Focal Point: What is one thing you are manifesting today?

```
┌─────────────────────────────────────────────────┐
│                                                 │
│                                                 │
│                                                 │
└─────────────────────────────────────────────────┘
```

What Actions will you take to manifest this?

_____
_____
_____
_____

Know Your Why: Why is what you are manifesting special? How will receiving it positively change you?

_____
_____
_____
_____

Your personal Affirmation/Declarations for the day. (Affirm 3-5 times a day)

_____
_____
_____

Manifesting Notes A.M.

Manifesting Notes P.M.

Manifesting Reflections

WEEK 10

You've come too far to give up now. God has already made a way for you!
What you are manifesting is ALREADY YOURS!

DON'T QUIT

Write a paragraph or two as if your next week has already happened!

"I attract to my life whatever I give my attention, energy and focus to, whether positive or negative."
– *Michael Losier*

Manifesting Your Best Life

Day: _____   Date: _____

Attitude of Gratitude: What are you thankful for today?

1. _____
2. _____
3. _____
4. _____

Today's Focal Point: What is one thing you are manifesting today?

```
┌─────────────────────────────────────────────────────────────────┐
│                                                                 │
│                                                                 │
│                                                                 │
└─────────────────────────────────────────────────────────────────┘
```

What Actions will you take to manifest this?

_____
_____
_____
_____

Know Your Why: Why is what you are manifesting special? How will receiving it positively change you?

_____
_____
_____
_____

Your personal Affirmation/Declarations for the day. (Affirm 3-5 times a day)

_____
_____
_____
_____

Manifesting Notes A.M.

Manifesting Notes P.M.

Manifesting Your Best Life

Day: _____   Date: _____

Attitude of Gratitude: What are you thankful for today?

1. _____
2. _____
3. _____
4. _____

Today's Focal Point: What is one thing you are manifesting today?

┌──┐
│   │
│   │
│   │
└──┘

What Actions will you take to manifest this?

_____
_____
_____
_____

Know Your Why: Why is what you are manifesting special? How will receiving it positively change you?

_____
_____
_____
_____

Your personal Affirmation/Declarations for the day. (Affirm 3-5 times a day)

_____
_____
_____
_____

Manifesting Notes A.M.

Manifesting Notes P.M.

Manifesting Your Best Life

Day: _____   Date: _____

Attitude of Gratitude: What are you thankful for today?

1. _____
2. _____
3. _____
4. _____

Today's Focal Point: What is one thing you are manifesting today?

_____

What Actions will you take to manifest this?

_____
_____
_____
_____

Know Your Why: Why is what you are manifesting special? How will receiving it positively change you?

_____
_____
_____
_____

Your personal Affirmation/Declarations for the day. (Affirm 3-5 times a day)

_____
_____
_____

Manifesting Notes A.M.

Manifesting Notes P.M.

Manifesting Your Best Life

Day: _____   Date: _____

Attitude of Gratitude: What are you thankful for today?

1. _____
2. _____
3. _____
4. _____

Today's Focal Point: What is one thing you are manifesting today?

┌──┐
│   │
│   │
│   │
└──┘

What Actions will you take to manifest this?

_____
_____
_____
_____

Know Your Why: Why is what you are manifesting special? How will receiving it positively change you?

_____
_____
_____
_____

Your personal Affirmation/Declarations for the day. (Affirm 3-5 times a day)

_____
_____
_____
_____

Manifesting Notes A.M.

Manifesting Notes P.M.

Manifesting Your Best Life

Day: _____   Date: _____

Attitude of Gratitude: What are you thankful for today?

1. _____
2. _____
3. _____
4. _____

Today's Focal Point: What is one thing you are manifesting today?

```
┌──────────────────────────────────────────────────────────┐
│                                                          │
│                                                          │
│                                                          │
│                                                          │
└──────────────────────────────────────────────────────────┘
```

What Actions will you take to manifest this?

_____
_____
_____
_____

Know Your Why: Why is what you are manifesting special? How will receiving it positively change you?

_____
_____
_____
_____

Your personal Affirmation/Declarations for the day. (Affirm 3-5 times a day)

_____
_____
_____
_____

Manifesting Notes A.M.

Manifesting Notes P.M.

Manifesting Your Best Life

Day: _____   Date: _____

Attitude of Gratitude: What are you thankful for today?

1. _____
2. _____
3. _____
4. _____

Today's Focal Point: What is one thing you are manifesting today?

```
┌─────────────────────────────────────────────┐
│                                             │
│                                             │
│                                             │
└─────────────────────────────────────────────┘
```

What Actions will you take to manifest this?

_____
_____
_____
_____

Know Your Why: Why is what you are manifesting special? How will receiving it positively change you?

_____
_____
_____
_____

Your personal Affirmation/Declarations for the day. (Affirm 3-5 times a day)

_____
_____
_____
_____

Manifesting Notes A.M.

Manifesting Notes P.M.

Manifesting Your Best Life

Day: _____   Date: _____

Attitude of Gratitude: What are you thankful for today?

1. _____
2. _____
3. _____
4. _____

Today's Focal Point: What is one thing you are manifesting today?

```
┌─────────────────────────────────────────────────┐
│                                                 │
│                                                 │
│                                                 │
└─────────────────────────────────────────────────┘
```

What Actions will you take to manifest this?

_____
_____
_____
_____

Know Your Why: Why is what you are manifesting special? How will receiving it positively change you?

_____
_____
_____
_____

Your personal Affirmation/Declarations for the day. (Affirm 3-5 times a day)

_____
_____
_____
_____

Manifesting Notes A.M.

Manifesting Notes P.M.

Manifesting Reflections

WEEK 11

It is open door season, and you are stepping into your increase! Name it.
Claim it.
Remember its already yours!

Write 5 things you have manifested so far.

"Whatever you hold in your mind on a consistent basis is exactly what you will experience in your life"
– Tony Robbins

Manifesting Your Best Life

Day: _____   Date: _____

Attitude of Gratitude: What are you thankful for today?

1. _____
2. _____
3. _____
4. _____

Today's Focal Point: What is one thing you are manifesting today?

```
┌─────────────────────────────────────────────────┐
│                                                 │
│                                                 │
│                                                 │
│                                                 │
└─────────────────────────────────────────────────┘
```

What Actions will you take to manifest this?

_____
_____
_____
_____

Know Your Why: Why is what you are manifesting special? How will receiving it positively change you?

_____
_____
_____
_____

Your personal Affirmation/Declarations for the day. (Affirm 3-5 times a day)

_____
_____
_____
_____

Manifesting Notes A.M.

Manifesting Notes P.M.

Manifesting Your Best Life

Day: _____   Date: _____

Attitude of Gratitude: What are you thankful for today?

1. _____
2. _____
3. _____
4. _____

Today's Focal Point: What is one thing you are manifesting today?

```
┌─────────────────────────────────────────────────┐
│                                                 │
│                                                 │
│                                                 │
└─────────────────────────────────────────────────┘
```

What Actions will you take to manifest this?

_____
_____
_____
_____

Know Your Why: Why is what you are manifesting special? How will receiving it positively change you?

_____
_____
_____
_____

Your personal Affirmation/Declarations for the day. (Affirm 3-5 times a day)

_____
_____
_____
_____

Manifesting Notes A.M.

Manifesting Notes P.M.

Manifesting Your Best Life

Day: _____   Date: _____

Attitude of Gratitude: What are you thankful for today?

1. _____
2. _____
3. _____
4. _____

Today's Focal Point: What is one thing you are manifesting today?

```
┌─────────────────────────────────────────────────────────┐
│                                                         │
│                                                         │
│                                                         │
└─────────────────────────────────────────────────────────┘
```

What Actions will you take to manifest this?

_____
_____
_____
_____

Know Your Why: Why is what you are manifesting special? How will receiving it positively change you?

_____
_____
_____
_____

Your personal Affirmation/Declarations for the day. (Affirm 3-5 times a day)

_____
_____
_____
_____

Manifesting Notes A.M.

Manifesting Notes P.M.

Manifesting Your Best Life

Day: _____   Date: _____

Attitude of Gratitude: What are you thankful for today?

1. _____
2. _____
3. _____
4. _____

Today's Focal Point: What is one thing you are manifesting today?

┌───┐
│   │
│   │
│   │
└───┘

What Actions will you take to manifest this?

_____
_____
_____
_____

Know Your Why: Why is what you are manifesting special? How will receiving it positively change you?

_____
_____
_____
_____

Your personal Affirmation/Declarations for the day. (Affirm 3-5 times a day)

_____
_____
_____
_____

Manifesting Notes A.M.

Manifesting Notes P.M.

Manifesting Your Best Life

Day: _____   Date: _____

Attitude of Gratitude: What are you thankful for today?

1. _____
2. _____
3. _____
4. _____

Today's Focal Point: What is one thing you are manifesting today?

```
┌─────────────────────────────────────────────────┐
│                                                 │
│                                                 │
│                                                 │
└─────────────────────────────────────────────────┘
```

What Actions will you take to manifest this?

_____
_____
_____
_____

Know Your Why: Why is what you are manifesting special? How will receiving it positively change you?

_____
_____
_____
_____

Your personal Affirmation/Declarations for the day. (Affirm 3-5 times a day)

_____
_____
_____
_____

Manifesting Notes A.M.

Manifesting Notes P.M.

Manifesting Your Best Life

Day: _____   Date: _____

Attitude of Gratitude: What are you thankful for today?

1. _____
2. _____
3. _____
4. _____

Today's Focal Point: What is one thing you are manifesting today?

```
┌─────────────────────────────────────────────────┐
│                                                 │
│                                                 │
│                                                 │
└─────────────────────────────────────────────────┘
```

What Actions will you take to manifest this?

_____
_____
_____
_____

Know Your Why: Why is what you are manifesting special? How will receiving it positively change you?

_____
_____
_____
_____

Your personal Affirmation/Declarations for the day. (Affirm 3-5 times a day)

_____
_____
_____
_____

Manifesting Notes A.M.

Manifesting Notes P.M.

Manifesting Your Best Life

Day: _____   Date: _____

Attitude of Gratitude: What are you thankful for today?

1. _____
2. _____
3. _____
4. _____

Today's Focal Point: What is one thing you are manifesting today?

[   ]

What Actions will you take to manifest this?

_____
_____
_____
_____

Know Your Why: Why is what you are manifesting special? How will receiving it positively change you?

_____
_____
_____
_____

Your personal Affirmation/Declarations for the day. (Affirm 3-5 times a day)

_____
_____
_____
_____

Manifesting Notes A.M.

Manifesting Notes P.M.

Manifesting Reflections

WEEK 12

Consistency allows God to move in our lives and on our behalf in a way that being inconsistent could never. You're so close! Continue to manifest your best!

Write 5 positive habits you will use next week to manifest your best week!

"When you are truly clear about what you want, the whole universe stands on tiptoe waiting to assist you in miraculous and amazing ways to manifest your dream or intention."
– Constance Arnold

Manifesting Your Best Life

Day: _____   Date: _____

Attitude of Gratitude: What are you thankful for today?

1. _____
2. _____
3. _____
4. _____

Today's Focal Point: What is one thing you are manifesting today?

```
┌─────────────────────────────────────────────────────────┐
│                                                         │
│                                                         │
│                                                         │
└─────────────────────────────────────────────────────────┘
```

What Actions will you take to manifest this?

_____
_____
_____
_____

Know Your Why: Why is what you are manifesting special? How will receiving it positively change you?

_____
_____
_____
_____

Your personal Affirmation/Declarations for the day. (Affirm 3-5 times a day)

_____
_____
_____
_____

Manifesting Notes A.M.

Manifesting Notes P.M.

Manifesting Your Best Life

Day: _____   Date: _____

Attitude of Gratitude: What are you thankful for today?

1. _____
2. _____
3. _____
4. _____

Today's Focal Point: What is one thing you are manifesting today?

```
┌─────────────────────────────────────────────────┐
│                                                 │
│                                                 │
│                                                 │
└─────────────────────────────────────────────────┘
```

What Actions will you take to manifest this?

_____
_____
_____
_____

Know Your Why: Why is what you are manifesting special? How will receiving it positively change you?

_____
_____
_____
_____

Your personal Affirmation/Declarations for the day. (Affirm 3-5 times a day)

_____
_____
_____
_____

Manifesting Notes A.M.

Manifesting Notes P.M.

Manifesting Your Best Life

Day: _____   Date: _____

Attitude of Gratitude: What are you thankful for today?

1. _____
2. _____
3. _____
4. _____

Today's Focal Point: What is one thing you are manifesting today?

```
┌─────────────────────────────────────────────────┐
│                                                 │
│                                                 │
│                                                 │
└─────────────────────────────────────────────────┘
```

What Actions will you take to manifest this?

_____
_____
_____
_____

Know Your Why: Why is what you are manifesting special? How will receiving it positively change you?

_____
_____
_____
_____

Your personal Affirmation/Declarations for the day. (Affirm 3-5 times a day)

_____
_____
_____
_____

Manifesting Notes A.M.

Manifesting Notes P.M.

Manifesting Your Best Life

Day: _____   Date: _____

Attitude of Gratitude: What are you thankful for today?

1. _____
2. _____
3. _____
4. _____

Today's Focal Point: What is one thing you are manifesting today?

┌───┐
│   │
│   │
│   │
└───┘

What Actions will you take to manifest this?

_____
_____
_____
_____

Know Your Why: Why is what you are manifesting special? How will receiving it positively change you?

_____
_____
_____
_____

Your personal Affirmation/Declarations for the day. (Affirm 3-5 times a day)

_____
_____
_____
_____

Manifesting Notes A.M.

Manifesting Notes P.M.

Manifesting Your Best Life

Day: _____   Date: _____

Attitude of Gratitude: What are you thankful for today?

1. _____
2. _____
3. _____
4. _____

Today's Focal Point: What is one thing you are manifesting today?

```
┌─────────────────────────────────────────────────┐
│                                                 │
│                                                 │
│                                                 │
│                                                 │
└─────────────────────────────────────────────────┘
```

What Actions will you take to manifest this?

_____
_____
_____
_____

Know Your Why: Why is what you are manifesting special? How will receiving it positively change you?

_____
_____
_____
_____

Your personal Affirmation/Declarations for the day. (Affirm 3-5 times a day)

_____
_____
_____
_____

Manifesting Notes A.M.

Manifesting Notes P.M.

Manifesting Your Best Life

Day: _____   Date: _____

Attitude of Gratitude: What are you thankful for today?

1. _____
2. _____
3. _____
4. _____

Today's Focal Point: What is one thing you are manifesting today?

```
┌─────────────────────────────────────────────────┐
│                                                 │
│                                                 │
│                                                 │
└─────────────────────────────────────────────────┘
```

What Actions will you take to manifest this?

_____
_____
_____
_____

Know Your Why: Why is what you are manifesting special? How will receiving it positively change you?

_____
_____
_____
_____

Your personal Affirmation/Declarations for the day. (Affirm 3-5 times a day)

_____
_____
_____
_____

Manifesting Notes A.M.

Manifesting Notes P.M.

Manifesting Your Best Life

Day: _____   Date: _____

Attitude of Gratitude: What are you thankful for today?

1. _____
2. _____
3. _____
4. _____

Today's Focal Point: What is one thing you are manifesting today?

```
┌─────────────────────────────────────────────────┐
│                                                 │
│                                                 │
│                                                 │
└─────────────────────────────────────────────────┘
```

What Actions will you take to manifest this?

_____
_____
_____
_____

Know Your Why: Why is what you are manifesting special? How will receiving it positively change you?

_____
_____
_____
_____

Your personal Affirmation/Declarations for the day. (Affirm 3-5 times a day)

_____
_____
_____
_____

Manifesting Notes A.M.

Manifesting Notes P.M.

Manifesting Reflections

WEEK 13

Congratulations! You've made it through the final week in this manifestation journal.
You set a goal and you stayed with it until the end! Enjoy the blessing filled harvest of your efforts!

What are your greatest takeaways from this 90-day experience and what are you most proud of about yourself?

Pray For It!

Believe It Will Happen!

Watch It Manifest!

-Jennifer Brown

Affirmations

1. I manifest abundance by expressing gratitude for what I already have in my life.
2. I am creatively inspired by the world around me.
3. My mind is full of brilliant ideas and today I chose to share them with the world.
4. I am worthy of a happy, healthy, and loving relationship.
5. My heart is healed, and I am ready for love.
6. Money comes to me in expected and unexpected ways.
7. I am attracting opportunities that bring forth generational blessings.
8. I release all trauma surrounding money; I am now creating a healthy money story.
9. I am in control of my thoughts, feelings, and the words I speak.
10. Every challenge in my life is an opportunity to grow and be a better me.

Write your own personal Affirmation.

_____
_____
_____
_____
_____
_____
_____
_____
_____
_____
_____

Scriptures

"You will succeed in whatever you choose to do, and light will shine on the road ahead of you."
Job 22:28 NLT

"The blessing of the Lord makes a person rich, and he adds no sorrow with it."
Proverbs 10:22 NLT

"But remember the Lord your God, for it is he who gives you the ability to produce wealth, and so confirms his covenant, which he swore to your ancestors, as it is today."
Deuteronomy 8:18 NIV

"Beloved friend, I pray that you are prospering in every way[a] and that you continually enjoy good health, just as your soul is prospering.[b]"
3 John 2 TPT

"Your words are so powerful that they will kill or give life, and the talkative person will reap the consequences."
Proverbs 18:21 TPT

"Don't be pulled in different directions or worried about a thing. Be saturated in prayer throughout each day, offering your faith-filled requests before God with overflowing gratitude. Tell him every detail of your life, then God's wonderful peace that transcends human understanding, will guard your heart and mind through Jesus Christ. Keep your thoughts continually fixed on all that is authentic and real, honorable, and admirable, beautiful, and respectful, pure, and holy, merciful and kind. And fasten your thoughts on every glorious work of God, praising him always. Put into practice the example of all that you have heard from me or seen in my life and the God of peace will be with you in all things."
Philippians 4:6-9 TPT

"Therefore I say unto you, what things soever ye desire, when ye pray, believe that ye receive them, and ye shall have them."
Mark 11:24 KJV

"Give generously, and generous gifts will be given back to you shaken down to make room for more. Abundant gifts will pour out upon you with such an overflowing measure that it will run over the top! Your measurement of generosity becomes the measurement of your return."
Luke 6:38 TPT

"And this is the confidence that we have in him, that, if we ask any thing according to his will, he heareth us: 15 And if we know that he hears us, whatsoever we ask, we know that we have the petitions that we desired of him."
1 John 5:14-15 KJV

Declarations

1. I declare unexpected blessings are coming my way. God is opening supernatural doors for me.
2. I declare that I am HEALED and walking in divine health.
3. I declared that unimaginable blessings are happening in my life right now. God's favor is raining down on me.
4. I declare Peace of Mind, increased faith and total trust in what God is doing in my life right now. I am birthing out every promise God has put in my heart.
5. I declare I will overcome every obstacle that comes my way I am full of divine strength and power.
6. I declare total restoration for all the years I feel like I made bad choices and missed opportunities thank you Lord that you have restored my time.
7. I declare Ephesians 3:20 over my life. God will do exceedingly abundantly above all that I ask or think. I am showered by God's favor.
8. I declare that I am in a new season of growth in my life, new opportunities presenting themselves to me now.
9. I declare I will steward well the gifts, talents, opportunities, and relationships that are in my life.
10. I declare I am a happy, healthy, wise, and walking into divine abundance in every area of my life.

Write your own personal Declaration.

_____
_____
_____
_____
_____
_____
_____
_____

Closing Prayer

I pray that the Father of glory, the God of our Lord Jesus Christ, would impart to you the riches of the Spirit of wisdom and the Spirit of revelation to know him through your deepening intimacy with him.

I pray that the light of God will illuminate the eyes of your imagination, flooding you with light, until you experience the full revelation of the hope of his calling —that is, the wealth of God's glorious inheritances that he finds in us, his holy ones!

I pray that you will continually experience the immeasurable greatness of God's power made available to you through faith. Then your lives will be an advertisement of this immense power as it works through you! This is the mighty power.

Ephesians 1:17-19 TPT

Manifesting Notes

Manifesting Notes

Manifesting Notes

Manifesting Notes

Manifesting Notes

Manifesting Notes

Manifesting Notes

Manifesting Notes

Manifesting Notes

Manifesting Notes

Manifesting Notes

Manifesting Notes

www.ingramcontent.com/pod-product-compliance
Lightning Source LLC
LaVergne TN
LVHW081550060526
838201LV00054B/1833